Better Diving

Better Diving

by Jennifer Gray

Photographs by Gary Gray

Kaye & Ward · London

With thanks to Pauline Baker
and Graham Topping who posed for
the photographs

First published in Great Britain by
Kaye & Ward Ltd.
Century House, 82/84 Tanner Street, London SE1 3PP
1981

Copyright © Kaye & Ward Ltd 1981

All Rights Reserved. No part of this publication may be reproduced, stored in a retrieval system, or transmitted, in any form or by any means, electronic, mechanical, photocopying, recording or otherwise, without the prior permission of the copyright owner.

ISBN 0 7182 1473 0

Printed in Great Britain by
Whitstable Litho Ltd.
Whitstable, Kent

Contents

1. **Introduction**   7
2. **Poolside Practices**   9
3. **Springboard Diving**   40
4. **Highboard Diving**   78
5. **Land Conditioning**   86
   Appendix   93

1 INTRODUCTION

In its brief history diving has changed dramatically.

When bathing first became fashionable, entry into the water was as sedate as possible. In swimming books written at the beginning of the twentieth century, simple plunging was mentioned and although diving was being introduced, it was not taken seriously. In 1902 Montague Holbein wrote, 'Plunging and diving are perhaps the finest amusements connected with swimming. The high dive may be termed, "a mere drop at a downward angle".' However, he still considered it quite dangerous, and wrote mainly of the disagreeable sensations that would be experienced.

Diving developed from the growth of aerial acrobatics and tumbling. Many of the early divers were gymnasts who discovered that water made a softer landing place than dry land. Trapezes and rings were hung over the water and acrobatics were performed from the apparatus into the water. Gradually the apparatus was discarded and diving then took place from a fixed platform.

At the beginning of the century, diving competitions were inaugurated. Initially they were for men only. It was thought to be most undignified for ladies. However, thoughts changed and ladies' diving was first included in the 1912 Olympic Games at which Britain's Belle White gained the bronze medal.

At first, all diving took place from fixed platforms or firmboards. Springboards were not introduced until the early 1920's. These early springboards were planks of wood which gave very little spring. They bore very little resemblance to the maxiflex metal alloy boards to be found in many diving pits today.

As with all sports, development and changes are continually taking place. Dives are now performed which were unthought of a few years ago. This improvement is due to the technology which is being utilised in the design of boards, a greater provision of facilities and, most importantly, the increased understanding and application of training techniques.

BEGINNING TO DIVE

It is never too early or too late to start to learn to dive, but obviously the earlier the start the more likelihood there is of achieving success. Before starting, it is essential that the potential diver is happy when swimming in deep water, not afraid of going under water and is prepared to show determination in performing the movements. Most minor knocks are caused by divers attempting movements in only a half-hearted manner. Success is more likely if one puts maximum effort into every movement.

There are many qualities which a would-be diver must possess, but one of the most important is the ability to repeat movements over and over again without becoming bored.

Clubs and classes may be found in many swimming pools, and from these classes, divers with any potential will usually be selected to undertake individual training. A good coach or teacher is important for future success. Remember that becoming a top class diver takes many years and requires total dedication. It does not happen overnight.

If you require advice about clubs in your area, contact the Amateur Swimming Association, Harold Fern House, Derby Square, Loughborough, Leicestershire.

2 POOLSIDE PRACTICES

Before diving, it is important always to ensure that the water is deep enough. It should be about 0.5 metre deeper than the diver with his arms fully stretched above his head.

The basic movements of diving are best learned from the poolside. From this position the flight time or time in the air is very short, but the advantages are that there are no timing problems as when using a springboard and it is not so far to get into the water. This is a great psychological advantage when learning new dives. A dive will not easily be learned simply by performing the whole skill. This 'have a go' method can lead to accidents. It is usually better to start with simple, basic practices on the poolside, gradually building up until the full dive can be attempted. However, when a longer flight time is required perform the dives initially from a board rather than the poolside.

For each of the dives described in this book, progressive practices are given. Never move on too quickly from one practice to the next. The diver should be able to perform each practice several times with consistent accuracy before progressing to the next stage.

Remember, it is easier to learn a movement correctly than to correct a fault.

BASIC INFORMATION

Dives are analysed under four headings, the stance, take-off, flight and entry.

The Stance

The stance, is the preparatory stage where the diver takes up an upright position either forwards or backwards on the board, depending on the dive to be performed. For running dives, the stance is a measured distance from the end of the board. This stance is exceptionally important as it not only creates the initial impression but also a good stance ensures that the body is in the correct position for take-off. The body should be in a comfortable, erect position, with the chest high, the head up and the eyes focused forwards. The pelvis should be tilted under and the stomach held firm. It is a very common mistake to stand with an arched back. This fault will cause the diver to swing the body down too vigorously and cause the dive to over rotate.

Take-off
The take-off is the next and most important part of any dive. At take-off, the line of flight is set. During the take-off, three movements must happen. Firstly the diver must gain his height. Height is only gained by pressing hard into the board and then, on the springboard, waiting for the board to lift the body into the air. On the firmboard, the diver must use his own spring to gain height. Good timing is essential for maximum height to be gained. The diver must wait for the board to lift him. Secondly rotation can only be created with a part of the body in contact with the board. Once in the air, the diver can speed up or slow down the rotation, but cannot create it. Thirdly the last and vital component of the take-off is the lean away from the end of the board. For safety it is essential that the diver gains some movement away from the end of the board, though it must be kept to a minimum. Movement away from the board is gained only at the expense of height and height is necessary for the diver to complete his movements and for the dive to look aesthetically pleasing.

Flight
The flight through the air is the next stage of the dive. During the flight the body may be carried in one of three recognised positions, straight, piked and tucked. In the *straight* position, the body is held firm, the head is in line with the trunk, the legs are together, ankles stretched and toes pointed. The position of the arms is optional, but they are usually held in a 'Y' or 'T'

1. The straight position. The body is held firm and straight. The position of the arms is optional.

position. For forward and inward dives the body is perfectly straight, whereas for backward and reverse dives there is some arch in the top of the spine.

In the *piked* position, the body is bent only at the hips so that the legs are straight at the knees and the feet are together and stretched. The position of the arms depends on the dive being performed, although technically the position is optional. For pike dives, the hands reach down to touch the front or sides of the extended feet. For fast rotating somersaults, the hands clasp behind the thighs so that the body is as compact as possible. The speed of rotation can be adjusted by bringing the trunk and the legs closer together. Remember, the more compact the body, the faster it will rotate. For slower rotating somersaults, the arms are held free, out to the sides of the body.

2. The pike position in which the body is bent only at the hips with the back and legs remaining straight. The position of the arms is optional.

The *tuck* is the fastest rotating position in which the body is as compact as possible, with the legs bent at the knees and hips, ensuring the knees and feet are together. The hands must grasp the lower legs with the elbows tucked into the sides. It is important that the head is not 'buried' in the knees or the diver will not be able to see where he is going.

When tucked, the diver rotates approximately four times faster than in the straight position.

3. The tuck position. The body is compact with the back rounded and the hands holding the lower legs.

Entry
The final part of the dive is the *entry* into the water, which should be as near to vertical as possible. It is safest to enter slightly short of the vertical. Though most dives require a head first entry it is also possible to enter dives feet first. Somersaults for example are not jumps when entry is made feet first. In head first entries, the hands make the initial 'hole'. They should be held firmly together to protect the head. The arms should be extended beyond the head. The top of the head enters next and is followed by the stretched, straight body. Muscle tension is required to keep the body in line. The dive is complete only after the feet have disappeared below the surface. For feet first entries, the body should be erect, with the head up and the body perfectly straight. The arms must be held close to the body.

There are two major faults that can occur during the entry. These are going short where the diver fails to achieve sufficient rotation and going over where too much rotation has been achieved.

THE PLAIN HEADER (4 - 8)

This is the first dive that should be mastered as it follows a 'natural' line of flight and with a slight bend at the hips the amount of rotation can be controlled. Remember, the tighter the body pikes, the faster it will rotate.

PROGRESSIVE PRACTICES

Spring Header
Stand in a semi-crouched position with the feet together and the toes gripping the edge of the pool. Bend the knees slightly and lean forward so the weight is over the toes. Stretch the arms upwards into a 'Y' position, keep the head in line with the trunk and focus on an object directly forward. From this stance, drive vigorously up through the hips and follow a curved flight into the water. During the flight, close the arms together to protect the head on entry. The entry should be about a metre from the side and as near vertical as possible. Think of two essential points – head down and hips up.

4. The diver starts in the 'Y' position, with the toes gripping the edge of the pool.

5. On take-off, the shoulders move forward and the diver drives up through the hips. Good extension through the knees, ankles and toes is essential.

The Plain Header

This is similar to the spring header, but starts with the diver in an upright position with the body straight and firm. Tilt the pelvis under and hold the stomach firm. A good stance is essential. From this firm position, push off strongly through the ankles and toes. On take-off pull in the stomach so that the body is in a slightly piked position. It is important after take-off to have good extension in the legs and feet and to bring the arms smoothly together to give a clean entry into the water. Take the dive right down to the bottom of the pool.

6. During the flight, the arms remain in the 'Y' position. The body is bent only at the hips.

7. The arms close firmly over the ears for entry. The pike in the body is reduced.

8. The entry into the water is slightly short of the vertical. By the time the feet have completely disappeared, the diver will be vertical.

9. An upright take-off is essential or the dive will over rotate.

10. The diver drives the hips above the head into a tight tuck position. The hands must grasp the shins.

THE FORWARD DIVE WITH TUCK

The forward dive with tuck is an easy dive to control. Because the tuck is a fast rotating position, the take-off must be more vertical than for the plain header or the dive will over rotate. The dive can be controlled by holding the tuck longer if the dive is going short or opening early if the dive is over rotating.

PROGRESSIVE PRACTICES

The Tuck Jump

Start in an upright position with the arms either stretched above the head or by the sides of the body. Spring high from the side and sharply bring the knees up to the chin so that the body is as compact as possible. Grasp the shins with the hands. Straighten quickly to enter the water feet first. It is important to keep the shoulders back and the head up.

11. The eyes focus on the point of entry whilst the body uncurls.

12. A clean, splash-free entry is desirable.

Forward Tuck Bomb

Start with the hands above the head, drive the hips high above the head and enter in a tuck position. This 'hips above head' position can be practised holding on to a rail or a high bench. Start holding the rail with both hands. Keep the elbows straight. Drive the hips up until they are above the head. Allow a teacher to catch the hips.

The Forward Dive with Tuck (9 - 12)

Start in an upright position with the arms stretched up close to the ears with the palms facing inwards. Drive the hips strongly up into the tuck position, bringing the hands down to clasp the shins. Keep the elbows neatly into the body. Allow the body to rotate until the hips are above the head and then stretch for entry. Maintain the stretched position until completely submerged.

13. From a stable back crouched position, the diver rolls back until off balance.

14. The diver then pushes back from the side.

THE BACK DIVE STRAIGHT

PROGRESSIVE PRACTICES

The Backward Jump
Start in a backward position with half the feet firmly on the bathside, and the arms stretched vertically above the head. The body should feel comfortable and balanced. Jump backwards keeping the head up and the chest high. Enter the water about 0.75 metre from the poolside.

The Back Roll (13)
Start in a backward crouch position with the feet at the edge of the pool. Grasp the knees, tuck the chin in and roll backwards. Keep in a tight ball.

The Back Pike Sit (14 - 15)
From the same starting position as the previous practice, start to roll back

15. Entry is hips first, a safe distance from the side.

and then push backwards stretching the legs. Keep the shoulders forward and reach for the toes. Enter the water hips first. This practice is to ensure the diver pushes away from the side and enters a safe distance from it. Once distance from the side is achieved, the diver should progress quickly to the next practice.

Water Practice
Start in the water, face the side and hold the rail or scum trough with both hands. Bring the feet up on to the wall close to the hands. From this curled up position drive backwards, throw the arms over the head and stretch the body along the surface of the water.

The next time, arch the back and try to perform a backward handstand on the bottom of the pool. It is important to press the hips upwards and stretch the legs. Ensure that the body is kept square throughout the whole movement. It is essential that this movement can be achieved before attempting the next stage.

Standing Back Dive

Stand in a backward stance with the arms in a 'Y' position. Focus on a point directly in front of the body. Lean slightly back, drive strongly upwards through the hips, press the chest high to the ceiling and look back for the water. Keep the arms in line with the body. If the head drops back too quickly and the arms swing too vigorously, then the dive will over rotate. Close the arms together for entry.

Crouched Back Dive

Start in a crouched position on the bathside. Start to roll backwards, push off strongly from the side and arch the back. At the same time, swing the arms over the head. Enter the water head first maintaining an arched position. Take the dive down to the bottom of the pool. Think of the movements – roll – push and arch.

16 - 20. From the crouched position, the diver rolls back, pushes hard from the side and then arches back for the water. The hands and head are pressed back to ensure a safe entry.

16.

17.

18.

19.

20.

21.   22.

21 - 24. The back pike sit is the preparation for the back dive piked from the board. The diver jumps high, lifts the feet up to the hands and enters hips first. It is important to keep the shoulders forward and the head up.

BACK DIVE PIKED

It is very difficult to perform a back dive piked from the bathside, but bathside lead up movements can be practised and then the diver can attempt the full movement from the board.

PROGRESSIVE PRACTICES

Back Pike Roll

Stand in a backward stance, keeping the legs straight, bend at the waist and

23.   24.

hold the ankles. Maintaining this piked position, roll backwards and sit in the water.

This practice can also be performed with a slight push.

Back Pike Sit (21 - 24)

Start in a backward stance. Drive strongly upwards, pull the stomach in firmly and bring the feet up to meet the hands. Keep the hands in front of the body so that they can always be seen. Maintain this position and enter the water piked.

This can also be practised on dry land. Jump high and bring one leg up to meet the hands. Land back on the take-off foot. Keep the shoulders forward and the head high.

Once the back pike sit from the bathside has been mastered, it is time to have a go at the full dive from a one metre springboard.

INWARD DIVE WITH TUCK

This dive is very similar to a forward dive with tuck except the diver stands backwards on the bathside and then rotates forward. It is important that the diver has 'had a go' at a forward dive with tuck before attempting the inward dive.

PROGRESSIVE PRACTICES

Inward Jump

Assume a backward stance with the shoulders well forward over the toes and the stomach pulled in and the hips out. Drive the hips and feet back towards the middle of the pool and enter the water feet first at a 45 degrees angle. For safety, keep the arms extended above the head.

25. The diver adopts a backward stance with the shoulders well over the toes.

26. On the take-off, the shoulders are kept over the toes and the hips are pressed out towards the middle of the pool.

27. Entry is at an angle of about 45°. For safety, the hands should be kept above the head.

Inward Tuck Bomb

Take up the same starting position. Drive the hips strongly backward and upward and grasp the shins. Try to enter head first in the tuck position. Keep the shoulders forward and think of chasing the knees round with the chin. The practice at the rail for the forward dive with tuck should also be used at this stage for the inward dive. Remember to drive down strongly with the arms as this helps to initiate rotation.

Once a head first bomb can be performed from the poolside it is time to try to dive from the board.

28. The diver stands with the hips pressed back and the shoulders over the toes.

29. The hips are driven up and back and the arms are swung down to the knees.

30. Entry is in a head first bomb.

FORWARD SOMERSAULT WITH TUCK

PROGRESSIVE PRACTICES

Crouched Roll
Start in a tight crouched position on the bathside. Grasp the shins, tuck the chin and roll in. Maintain the tucked position until the body is fully submerged. Try the same movement giving a slight push.

31. From the low crouched position, the diver grasps the shins, tucks the head in and overbalances. No push is required.

32. The diver rolls in for a head first entry.

Semi-crouched Somersault

Assume a low semi-crouched position with the arms above the head, but with the elbows bent so that the hands are slightly behind the head. Swing the arms over the head, at the same time tuck the knees tightly up to the chest. Keep the head forward and the chin pressed in. Try to enter the water in a sitting position.

Progress gradually through a less crouched starting position until standing. It is now time to try the full somersault.

33. The diver adopts a balanced stance with the arms above the head. They are ready to swing strongly down to help to create the rotation.

34. The diver pushes from the side and tucks as tightly as possible.

Forward Somersault with Tuck (35 - 37)

Start in an upright position and, keeping the shoulders well forward, perform a similar movement to that of the semi-crouched position. Think of 'chasing the knees round with the chin'.

In competition, it is rare to see a diver perform a single somersault from a board. One and a half somersaults are usually performed. From the poolside it is better to hang on to the tuck and try to enter head first. If one continually comes out of the tuck early one will get into the habit of doing this and may find it difficult to perform one and a half somersaults later.

35. The diver starts in an upright take-off with the arms stretched above the head, palms facing inwards.

36. The arms are driven strongly downward, the hips upward and, at the same time, the diver adopts a tight tuck position.

37. This tight position is maintained until entry.

REVERSE DIVE STRAIGHT

This appears to be a difficult dive as the diver starts in a forward stance and then rotates back towards the board. Therefore, during the flight through the air the diver is unable to see the water.

From the poolside, it is difficult to perform the dive from a two footed take-off as there is insufficient time to rotate fully. The lead up practices are therefore usually started with a one footed or kicking take-off. With learner divers it may be an advantage for them to wear a Tee shirt. It certainly reduces the sting if the diver lands on his back and also gives him the confidence to try a little harder. However, beginners should not wear shirts for too long or they will never have a go without one.

PROGRESSIVE PRACTICES

Reverse Jump

Start with one foot on the edge of the pool with the toes gripping the side and the other foot back from the side. The shoulders should be directly over the front foot, with the arms hanging down slightly behind the hips. Vigorously swing the arms and back leg forwards and upwards and enter with both feet together at an angle sloping towards the side of the pool.

One Footed Entry

It is now time to try and gain more rotation. This can be achieved by starting in the same position as for a reverse jump. Imagine that there is a football directly in front and try to kick it straight up to the ceiling above the head. Swing the arms strongly forwards and upwards to initiate the rotation. Enter the water at about a 45 degrees angle with one leg pointing high up to the ceiling about 0.75 metre away from the side. The stronger the kick the more rotation will be achieved.

Once this movement has been mastered and the diver is really kicking high with confidence, the next stage is to try to get the head in the water first.

38. The diver starts with one foot gripping the side. The body is bent slightly forwards and the arms are behind the hips.

39. The back foot, together with the arms, is swung strongly forwards and upwards. It's just like kicking a football up to the ceiling.

40. Entry is foot first, with the arm above the head and one foot up to the ceiling.

Reverse Dive - One Footed Take-off (41 - 46)

Prior to attempting the whole movement, the diver must experience kicking high and then arching back. This arching movement can be added to the previous practice after entry into the water. After entering the water feet first, arch the back, press the hips high and describe a complete circle under water, and surface towards the middle of the pool.

This intermediary practice allows the diver to attempt all the required movements without worrying about landing flat.

41.

42.

43.

44.

It is now time to attempt the complete dive. Start as for the previous practices, swing the arms and legs hard and arch the back and try and enter the water head first. It is essential that both legs are lifted high and the back is strongly arched. The greater the arch the easier it is to rotate. It may help if there is a fixed object behind the diver to look back at.

Some divers may prefer to attempt this dive from a two footed take-off. This is quite acceptable as from the springboard a two footed take-off is required.

Once the diver is able to enter head first from the bathside, with a little confidence he will be able to transfer the movement to the board.

41 - 46. The diver kicks hard, swings the arms vigorously above the head and looks back for the water. The bent legs help to give the diver rotation.

45.

46.

REVERSE DIVE PIKED

A dive in a piked position is far easier to control than in a straight position. If the diver is over rotating then he is able to come out of the pike early and if he is going short or under rotating then it is possible to hold the pike longer. It is therefore far more common for a diver, once he has experienced the reverse movement, to change the dive to the piked position.

It is impossible for the diver to complete a reverse dive piked from the bathside, but lead up practices should be experienced before trying the dive from the one metre board.

PROGRESSIVE PRACTICES

Pike Jump
This is similar to the forward jump with tuck, but instead of bringing the knees up to the chin, bring the feet up to the horizontal and the hands down to meet the toes. Straighten the body before entry into the water. It is essential that the legs remain straight throughout the jump.

Reverse Pike Jump
From the two footed take-off, drive the feet up higher into the air, straighten out and enter the water leaning back towards the side of the pool.

Reverse Pike Sit
This is similar to the back pike sit except that the practice starts facing the water. Strongly drive the legs up to meet the hands, which should remain high and slightly in front of the face.

To help lift the legs, pull in strongly on the stomach muscles. Keep the body piked and enter on the buttocks.

These are the only practices that the diver can perform from the bathside as there is insufficient time to open out to get a head first entry. When this has been mastered, it is time to try the whole dive from the board.

FORWARD DIVE HALF TWIST (47 - 49)

This is probably the most difficult of all the basic dives to perfect as it requires rotation around two different axes. It requires rotation in the forward direction, the same as for the forward dive and also requires rotation along the length of the body. The diver starts as if for a forward dive and then enters the water the same as for the back dive straight. It is essential, therefore, that the diver is able to perform both a forward dive straight and a back dive straight before attempting this dive.

47. The diver starts in the spring header position with the knees slightly bent and the body bent at the hips.

48. During take-off, one arm is pressed across the body and the diver arches.

49. Entry into the water is the same as for a back dive.

PROGRESSIVE PRACTICES

Half Twist Jumps
Half twist jumps should first be performed to establish the most comfortable direction for twisting. It does not always follow that a right handed diver will use his right arm to twist. Perform half twist jumps in both directions. Entry should be with the diver facing the bathside. Twist by pressing one arm across the body. Keep the arms high and in the 'Y' position.

Water Work
Much of the preliminary work for this dive can be done in the water.

Start with push and glides. Push away from the bathside and stretch along the surface of the water. Hold the stretched position until the body stops. Ensure that the arms are stretched beyond the head.

The next time, trying to keep the arms close to the head, push, glide and roll over on the back. Keep the body 'wriggle' to a minimum.

Next, immediately after turning onto the back, press the head back and the hips up and try to go down to the bottom of the pool into a backward handstand position. Press immediately into the arch position.

From the Poolside
Start in the spring header position with the knees bent, the body leaning slightly forward and the arms in a 'Y' position.

Imagine there is a fly in the water. Dive, use one arm to flick the fly out of the way, arch the back hard and look back to see if the fly has disappeared. This is one way that the half twist dive can be attempted for the first time. Another method is to imagine that you are driving a car down the road and the water is a brick wall. Hold the steering wheel in both hands, dive off and then firmly turn the wheel to avoid hitting the wall. Remember to enter the water in a back arched position the same as for a back dive straight.

These are two picturesque ways of teaching the dive which otherwise is quite difficult to explain.

The laws governing a twist dive state 'that the twist must not be manifestly taken from the board'. This means that although the twist is initiated whilst the feet are still in contact with the side, it must not be obvious to an observer.

FORWARD DIVE HALF TWIST STRAIGHT

The dive is started in the 'Y' position. On take-off, press one arm across the body towards the corner of the pool. This arm should be kept high and point to where the walls meet the ceiling. Look along this extended arm and then drop the head back ready for entry into the water. At take-off, press the hips in and tighten the buttocks. Try to follow a smooth curve into the water.

3 SPRINGBOARD DIVING

In Chapter 2 the basic dives were covered from the bathside. The main reason for learning dives from the bathside is so that they can be transferred safely onto the board. Before transferring the dives it is essential that the diver learns to use the springboard. For competitions, two different heights of springboards are used and these are the boards found in most pools. They are one or three metres from the surface of the water. Modern springboards are exceptionally flexible and this flexibility can be controlled by adjusting the fulcrum. The fulcrum is adjusted by turning the wheel at the side of the board. By pushing the wheel towards the front of the board, the board becomes effectively 'shorter' and firmer. It has a much faster recoil. This fulcrum position is used mostly by young, light, inexperienced divers. It is also used by divers learning new dives as it is easier to control.

When the fulcrum is moved towards the rear pivot, the board becomes much more difficult to control. It becomes more flexible and the timing of the recoil is slower. The diver has to learn to wait for this recoil. If used correctly, however, it can give the diver tremendous height.

Dives can be performed from either a standing or a running take-off, but the running one is most commonly used as it gives the diver more height and thus more time in the air.

THE RUNNING SPRINGBOARD TAKE-OFF

This take-off is wrongly named as it is not a run but a controlled walk along the board. It consists of at least three paces followed by a high leap or hurdle step, landing with both feet together on the end of the board. It is essential that during these movements the diver stays balanced and synchronises his movements with the movement of the board or his flight will not be projected along the desired pathway. The running take-off is a complex movement to learn and requires considerable practice. But remember, the take-off is the most important part of any dive so practice of this movement is never wasted. It is possible to learn this movement away from the pool.

PROGRESSIONS TO LEARNING
THE RUNNING SPRINGBOARD TAKE-OFF (50 - 53)

First decide off which leg you must hop to give the most height. Hop up and down on both legs to decide which feels most comfortable and gives the most height.

Draw a line on the ground which represents the end of the springboard. Stand back two paces from this line. Step forward with the driving leg and then jump forward onto two feet to land on the end of the board. During the movement (without dropping the head) watch the end of the board. Repeat the movement, but this time drive the back leg through into a high hurdle position (photograph 51). At this stage, leave the arms by the sides and concentrate on keeping the body erect, getting the knee high and the toes pointed. Ensure that the hurdle step travels forward onto the end of the board.

Now try to co-ordinate the arm movements with those of the legs. At the end of the last step forward ensure the arms are slightly behind the hips. As the knee swings forward, raise the arms forwards and upwards until they are above the head in a 'Y' position. Keep the movements synchronised. As the knee goes up, the arms go up. On landing on the board, swing the arms down sideways to depress the board. From here, continue the movement forwards and upwards and jump high as if jumping into water. This complete movement should be performed smoothly and without hesitation. The final upward movement of the arms and body will eventually coincide with the upward movement of the board. During this final jump, lift the head and look up.

Practise this one step, hurdle and jump into the water both from the poolside and then from the one metre springboard. Before using the

50. The diver presses hard into the board with the leading foot.

51. The back leg is carried forwards and upwards into the hurdle position and the arms swing above the head.

springboard, push the fulcrum forward so that the board is as firm as possible. During these early practices keep the movements off the board to a jump. The hurdle step and take-off are enough to concentrate on.

Now take three paces before the hurdle. Measure out the paces and mark the starting position on the board. There are usually numbers or dots on the side of the board which can be used to mark the starting position. Stand

52. The feet come together in the air.

53. The diver lands with both feet together on the end of the board.

upright with the body relaxed, but firm, still maintaining a high head position. Watch the end of the board. Take three normal heel and toe steps forward and then drive down firmly with the front foot into the hurdle step. Keep the body balanced. Complete the movement as for the previous practice. Practise this movement until it can be performed with fluency. Remember, it will be impossible to perform a good dive without a good take-off.

STANDING SPRINGBOARD TAKE-OFF

This take-off is used for both forward and backward rotating dives. Again, good timing is essential.

Start with the body upright and balanced with the arms by the sides. Lift the arms sideways until they are in a 'Y' position above the head. At the same time, raise the body onto the balls of the feet. Without hesitation, swing the arms down, slightly behind the hips, bend the knees and then continue the movement forwards and upwards. Remember, as the arms go up, the body goes up.

This movement can also be learned away from the pool. Practise it in front of a mirror so that the movements can be seen accurately. It can also be performed off a low bench onto the floor. By practising off a bench, which represents the board, the diver is able to see if the body is perfectly balanced. Keep the arms moving smoothly and rhythmically.

Remember, the shoulders should be kept over the balls of the feet throughout the arm swing. Any backward lean will result in the body being thrown out to the middle of the pool. Minimal travel away from the board is required.

THE FORWARD DIVE

The forward dive can be performed in any of the three basic positions. That is straight, piked or with tuck.

It is probably best to start by learning the dive in the piked position, as this is fairly easy to control.

Forward Jump Piked

From the poolside, start by learning the forward jump in a piked position. Start in an upright position with the hands by the sides. Ensure that the toes are gripping the edge. Drive strongly forwards and upwards with the arms and, as the feet push from the side, drive them up to meet the hands. Keep the back and head up. In the pike position, the legs should be parallel to the surface of the water. Bring the legs smartly down ready for a foot first entry.

Pike Bomb

Start as for the pike jump. If preferred, the hands may be extended above the head. On take-off, drive the hips above the head and press the feet forward into the pike position. Maintain the pike for the entry. The rail practice of getting the hips above the head is also a useful exercise. This time keep the legs straight. It is possible to perform a forward dive piked from the poolside, but for the novice diver the extra height gained by starting from the one metre board is advantageous.

From the Board

Start as for the previous practice. Drive the hips up, bring the hands down to reach the feet and then press the feet up ready for a head first entry. Once the basic movement has been attempted it should now be refined, thinking of the following points.

At take-off, ensure that the body is leaving the board almost vertically. Drive through with the arms and do not be in too much of a hurry to get into the piked position. Push the hips up above the head and press the feet slightly forward, bringing the hands down to touch the front or sides of the feet. From this position, rotate slightly and then lift the legs to the vertical position. Open the arms sideways and squeeze them together above the head for entry. Keep the stomach firm throughout and ensure a fully extended position for entry. Remember that the dive is only complete after the feet have submerged. Maintain the fully stretched position until the bottom of the pool is reached.

THE FORWARD DIVE STRAIGHT (54 - 57)

This is a far more difficult dive to perform as the angle of take-off is critical if an accurate entry is to be achieved. It has a higher degree of difficulty and therefore if performed well is a better dive to be used in competition.

The dive used to be referred to as a swallow dive and was executed in a hollow back or arched position. It is now, as the name suggests, performed in a straight position, with the stomach and back held firm and only the head raised.

54. The diver watches the end of the board. A good take-off is essential.

55. As the feet leave the board, the chest and arms are lifted high and the feet are pressed up behind the board.

To achieve a streamlined and graceful position, at take-off reach high with the arms and then quickly bring them into a 'T' position, so that they are in line with the shoulders. As the feet leave the board, look up at a fixed point directly ahead and then stretch hard and hold this firm body and arm position until just prior to entry. Then squeeze the arms together. The body should line up just short of the vertical since, by the time the feet have

56. The body is held firm throughout the flight. The arms are held in a 'T' position.

57. The firm straight body position is maintained as the arms close together for entry.

disappeared below the surface, the true vertical position will have been reached. This method of lining up for entry should be used for all dives.

It is important that throughout the dive there is as little body and arm movement as possible. The dive should appear to 'hang' in mid-air as this feeling will give the impression that the diver has achieved a longer time in the air.

BACK DIVE STRAIGHT

Before taking the dive onto the springboard, ensure that you are entering short from the poolside. There are several ways that it can be transferred to the board.

Back Fall (58 - 62)

Push the fulcrum forwards. Stand in an upright position with the arms locked above the head. Keep the body firm and straight. This practice requires no push from the board. Keeping the feet in contact with the board, fall back, look back for the water and stretch. Very little arch is required to get in head first. This is the safest method of transferring the dive.

58. The diver starts in an upright position, with the body firm and the arms locked above the head.

59. Keeping the body perfectly straight, the diver falls backwards.

60. The feet stay in contact with the board for as long as possible. The diver looks back for the water and the back slightly arches.

61.

62. The diver continues to look back until entry is achieved.

Crouched Back Dive

It is possible to go back to the crouched back dive as practised on the poolside. Roll back, push up high and then stretch the dive down to the bottom of the pool. Keep the eyes focused forwards and the head in line with the body. Remember you have a little more time, so do not swing the arms and the head back too vigorously.

Back Dive (63 - 68)

Starting with the arms above the head in the 'Y' position, try the full dive. Drive up through the legs and hips, press the chest high and look back for the water. Entry should be about a metre from the end of the board and should be slightly short of the vertical.

The diver is now ready to try the dive with an arm swing. This arm swing will help to give the diver more height and therefore more time in the air. With more time, the diver does not need to rush the movements and the dive will look more graceful.

63 - 64. The arms swing vigorously down and through. The body is kept well balanced over the end of the board. Notice that the shoulders are directly over the toes.

63.

64.

65 - 66. The arms continue to swing above the head and as the feet leave the board the chest is pressed high and the arms spread into a 'T' position.

65.

66.

During the final arm swing, pull the stomach in firmly and allow the shoulders to move slightly back behind the end of the board. This backward shoulder travel ensures a safe distance from the board and also starts to create the rotation which is essential to the dive.

As the body leaves the board in a stretched position, keep the head up and start to bring the feet up towards the hands. Keep the hands in front of the head so that they can clearly be seen. In the pike position, the hands should touch the pointed toes. Maintain this pike until the legs are vertical and then keep the legs pressed high whilst the body opens backwards for the entry. The arms should be opened sideways and then brought together above the head if a fully controlled dive is to be achieved. This stretched body position should be held until the feet are submerged. Throughout the dive, remember to keep the legs straight and the toes pointed.

69. The diver reaches high on take-off.

70. The stomach is held firm and the feet press up; towards the hands.

71. In the pike position, the hands touch the front or sides of the feet.

72. The hands open sideways and the body is lowered back for a vertical entry.

73. The arms press against the ears for a firm entry.

REVERSE DIVE STRAIGHT

The first attempts at this dive from the board can either be made from a one or a two footed take-off. If the final practice from the bathside has been from a one footed take-off, then it is more usual to do the same.

Make the board as firm as possible by pushing the fulcrum forward.

Perform the dive exactly the same as from the poolside. It is essential that as much effort is put into the dive as from the bathside. The extra height gives the diver very little extra time in the air.

Once the diver is confident, a two footed take-off can be used. Use either a simple forward and upward arm swing or a a standing springboard take-off. Remember to press the chest high and look back for the water.

74. As the feet leave the board, the body is fully extended with the back slightly arched.

More height will be achieved if a running springboard take-off is used.

During the final drive from the board, reach up with the hands, keep the head up and the chest high. The movement is then very similar to the back dive straight. Pull the shoulders back and move the arms down into the 'T' position. As the body leaves the board, feel as though the hips and legs are moving forwards and upwards. At the top of the dive, look back for the water and spot the point of entry. During the downward part of the flight, close the arms together and stretch the body for the entry. During the flight, the top of the spine should be arched and then this arch is reduced as the diver stretches for entry.

75. The arms are lowered into a 'T' position. Pauline shows them a little too low. The head is pressed back to look for entry.

76. The body follows a graceful curve until the point of entry is spotted.

77. The arms start to close together and the arch in the back is reduced.

78. As the hands touch the water, the body is almost straight.

THE REVERSE DIVE PIKED (79 - 84)

As for the back dive piked, there are no build up practices from the board.

As the feet give their final push into the board, swing the arms strongly forwards and upwards to a position just in front of the face. Keep the chest lifted high and the shoulders pressed back. Press the feet strongly up to meet the hands and keep the eyes focused forwards. Hold the pike position until the legs are vertical and then open sideways into a stretched vertical entry.

This dive may first be performed from a standing take-off, or if the diver is confident, a running one may be used.

79 - 84. The reverse dive piked is very similar to the back dive piked. On take-off, the arms reach high, the feet are lifted to the hands and then the diver opens sideways for a vertical entry.

79.

80.

81.

82.

83.

84.

INWARD DIVE

The diver should first be confident at leaving the board backwards before this dive should be attempted. If back jumps are necessary then return to the final poolside practice of trying to get the head in before attempting the inward dive.

Start with as firm a board as possible. Stand with the arms stretched above the head in a relatively close position. The shoulders should be over the toes and the diver should feel confident. If the diver is hesitating and wobbly in the stance then the dive could become dangerous.

From this upright stance, strongly drive the hips up above the head and tuck tightly. Swing the arms down to grasp the shins. At this early stage it does not matter if the entry into the water is head first in a tuck position. As more height and more confidence are gained, the diver will have time to open out and stretch for entry. An 'out' may be essential for the first attempts at opening.

It is a very common mistake to twist from the board during the take-off. This is usually caused by fear of hitting the board and if it does occur, return to the early poolside practices until confidence is gained.

Once the diver can perform the dive in a tucked position then a pike should be attempted. This dive has a higher degree of difficulty.

INWARD DIVE PIKED

The movements in this dive are very similar to those in a forward dive piked, so it is essential that this dive has first been mastered. Before attempting the dive from the board, return to the poolside and try some inward pike drops. These are similar to the inward tuck drops, but the legs remain straight throughout. From the upright stretched position, drive the hips up, press the hands down to the feet and keep the legs straight. Enter hands and feet together in a piked position.

From the Board (85 - 89)

At take-off, keep the head and shoulders high, reach high with the arms and drive the hips up above the head. The feeling should be of the shoulders remaining in the same place whilst the hips rise. Press the feet forwards into the pike position. Rotate until the feet are just behind the hips and then lift the legs and feet into line with the body for entry. Keep the stomach firm and open the arms sideways to the closed position above the head.

It is essential that the head and chest are kept high during the take-off or the diver will be close to the board and the dive will probably over rotate.

85. The diver presses hard into the board.

86. As the feet leave the board, the arms reach high and the hips are driven **upward** and backward.

87. In the pike position, the hands reach for the toes. This position is held until the feet are behind the hips.

88. The arms open sideways and the feet are pressed above the head.

89. The diver stretches hard for a vertical entry.

FORWARD DIVE HALF TWIST (90 - 94)

One of the best methods of learning the forward dive half twist is from the one metre board. Start in a pike fall position with the arms in a 'Y' and the eyes focusing on the point of entry. Turn one shoulder so that the hand points towards that entry point. Over balance and push the shoulder forward, keeping the hand in line with the entry point. Bring the hips into line so that the body arches and bring the back hand round to the hand pushing for entry. Drop the head back and line up the body for a back dive entry. The practice is performed without any push from the board.

The Dive

The take-off for this dive must be the same as for the forward dive straight, but at the moment of take-off the twist must be started. The rules of the dive

90. The diver is square on take-off.

state that the twist must not be seen to be taken from the board, so this movement should be as unobtrusive as possible.

As the body leaves the board, spread the arms in a 'T' position. Press one shoulder back and look along the forward arm. Arch the back slightly. Look for the point of entry and then close the arms together and stretch for an entry which is similar to that of a back dive straight. Remember, close the arms slightly behind the head. The amount of twist will depend on the movement of the arms and body at take-off, but can be controlled during the flight. The speed of twist can be slowed by opening the arms wide or speeded up by closing the arms towards the body. Accuracy at take-off is required to ensure that the correct amount of forward movement is obtained as well as the correct amount of twist.

91. The arms spread wide into a 'T' position.

92. The diver presses one shoulder back and looks along the forward arm.

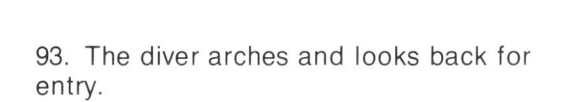

93. The diver arches and looks back for entry.

94. The arms close together. By the time the diver reaches the water, the entry will be vertical.

THE FORWARD ONE AND A HALF SOMERSAULT

This is probably one of the easiest of the somersault dives and is usually the first to be taught.

From the outset, attempt a forward one and a half somersaults rather than a single somersault. If the diver becomes used to entering the water feet first, he may find it difficult to transfer later to a head first entry.

Use a running springboard take-off. As the feet leave the board, reach up with the arms and drive the hips up above the head, swing the arms downward and bring the hands down to grasp the shins. It is this downward swing of the arms which helps to create the rotation. Maintain this tightly tucked position until the point of entry can be seen. Stretch out sharply into an extended position ready for entry.

The dive can also be performed in the piked position. The technique is similar, but the legs remain straight throughout.

FORWARD ONE AND A HALF SOMERSAULT WITH ONE TWIST (95- - 100)

This is the most difficult of the dives we have looked at as it combines somersaulting and twisting movements. The twisting technique used in this dive is different to that seen in the forward dive half twist as no twist must be taken from the board.

95.

96. On take-off, the hips are driven above the head into an open piked somersault.

97. The diver opens out for the twist. . .

98. and then repikes for the entry.

99. The piked position is held until the diver is almost vertical.

100. The diver then stretches for entry.

Open Pike Somersault

This is the first progression to learning the complete dive. Perform a single somersault in a pike position. Hold the arms out to the sides of the body in an open pike.

Develop the open pike somersault by pushing the arms up above the head and keeping them high throughout the movement. Drive the hips up strongly on take-off and then come out of the pike early so that the last part of the somersault is performed in the straight position.

Open Pike Somersault with One Twist

The next stage is to add the twist. First decide which is the best direction in which to twist. This can be established by trying a straight jump with one twist. Twist by pulling one hand back and behind the head and pull back on the same shoulder. At the same time, wrap the other arm across the body. Once the direction of twist has been established, it can be added to the previous movement.

The timing of the twist is important. It should occur as the diver 'kicks' out of the pike. It is essential that the stretching and twisting movements are sharp and precise.

One Pike Somersault with One Twist and Repike

At the end of the twisting movement, spread the arms wide into a 'T' position and then repike.

From the one metre board, a head and feet together entry will be most usual.

The dive is most easily achieved from the three metre board, but with practice it is possible to achieve a head first entry from the one metre board.

The position during the flight through the air is called the free position as it combines two of the basic body positions. Although it is called the free position, the component parts must conform to the rules related to the individual body positions, so that in the pike the body must be bent only at the hips, with the legs straight and the toes pointed. In the free position, it is possible to combine all three of the basic body positions.

4 HIGHBOARD DIVING

For competitive highboard or firmboard diving, three different heights of boards are used. These are 5 metres, 7.5 metres and 10 metres high. Other heights of firmboards may be used in school or club competition, but for national events only the three boards stated are allowed.

Looking down from the board, it appears to be a very long way. This distance is made greater as the surface of the water is not always distinguishable and it may be the surface of the water which is being observed. Sprays or jets of water are used to disturb the surface so it can be clearly seen.

The time in the air or flight time is not very much more from the ten metre board than from a good take-off from a three metre springboard. From the springboard the diver would take 1.50 seconds before reaching the water and 1.75 seconds from the ten metre board. The major difference is the speed at which the diver actually hits the water. From the ten metre board, the diver will be travelling at over 30 miles per hour by the time the water is reached. For this reason, good entry techniques are essential. Remember on entry, hold the hands firmly together, squeeze the arms over the ears, hold the stomach firm and stretch until completely submerged. The inability to hold this position will result in headaches and bruised shoulders.

Entries can be practised in several different ways.

Sitting Dives
Adopt a sitting position on the end of the board. Stretch the legs out in front, keep the back straight, the head up and hold the board close to the

body. From this comfortable position, press up on the hands so that the weight of the body is taken off the board, lean forward, push off with the hands and then just before the body is vertical, unpike and stretch for entry.

Practise first off the low boards and gradually work higher. Do not progress to the higher board until short entries can be consistently achieved.

Tucked Sitting Dives
A similar dive can be achieved from the sitting position. Start in a compact tucked position very close to the end of the board. Grasp the shins tightly and look along the shins to the point of entry. Maintaining this compact position, roll forward, and then, as with the previous practice, stretch for entry.

These two practices are ideal for the novice diver as the stance is a little closer to the water. It does not seem quite so far to go.

As confidence grows, build up to a pike fall.

Pike Fall
Start in a pike position, with the toes gripping the edge, the body bent sharply at the hips and the arms held in a 'Y' position with the eyes looking at the point of entry.

Roll forward, gradually unpike and then stretch for entry.

Forward Dive with Tuck
This is probably the first dive that should be taken onto the highboard, because it can be most easily controlled.

Start with the arms stretched directly above the shoulders with the palms turned to face each other. Drive the hips high and stretch for entry.

Remember - do not progress to a higher board until a short entry can be consistently achieved.

Take-offs
Firmboard take-offs differ considerably from those used on the springboard. It is pointless the diver waiting for the board to give lift. The diver has to use his 'natural' spring to get height from the board. The recoil of a

springboard also drives the diver slightly away from the end of the board, but this does not happen on a firmboard. Although all dives must be taken up, they must also be taken slightly out, so a little more lean is essential.

The other major difference between the two boards is that a new group of dives, the armstand group may be used and in this group take-off is from the hands rather than the feet.

Standing Forward Take-off

There are several different arm swings which may be used from the standing position. The one used depends on the dive being performed and also the diver's preference. The stance must be with the arms stretched directly above the head or with them held neatly by the sides.

From the arms extended position, the diver may simply adopt the technique used when learning dives from the bathside and keep the arms above the head throughout the take-off.

From the side position, an identical armswing to that used on a springboard may be adopted or the diver may omit the initial sideways armswing and drive the arms forwards and upwards into the dive.

Remember, whichever armswing is used, the diver must drive strongly from the board, getting strong extension through the knees, ankles and finishing with the toes. These take-offs can be practised firstly as land drills and then from the poolside into jumps.

Running Take-offs

There are two very different running movements which are used depending on the dive to be performed.

The two footed take-off is used for forward rotating dives and the one footed take-off is most commonly used for reverse dives. This one footed technique is very similar to the one used for learning the reverse dive from the poolside.

The Two Footed Take-off

The rules governing the take-off are identical to those for the springboard. A minimum of four contacts with the board must be made. The run must be both smooth and confident and because of the necessity for the diver to get high from the board, it is performed at a faster pace than from the springboard. It is a controlled run. The arms are either held close to the body or swing parallel to the line of the run.

The hurdle step is modified to a low jump onto the end of the board with emphasis on the final drive up.

The One Footed Take-off
This is performed at a much slower pace and is a controlled walk. After four contacts with the board, the rear leg and arms are swung forwards and upwards to gain height, rotation and distance from the board. The degree of swing depends on the dive to be performed. For a reverse dive straight, the diver steps off the end, whereas for a reverse two and a half somersaults, a vigorous kick is required.

Armstand Take-offs
It is a waste of valuable pool time to practise armstand balance positions from the board. These should be practised anywhere there is sufficient room to kick the legs up without doing damage.

There are several different methods of attaining the handstand position and the diver should experiment to see which suits his requirements. Whichever method is used, the diver must attain a perfectly balanced position with the body held in line.

Kick up
Draw a line on the ground which represents the end of the board. Place the hands on the ground, shoulder width apart so that the fingers are just touching the line. The fingers should be slightly flexed so that they can drive from the board. Ensure that the arms are straight and vertical and that the shoulders are directly above them. Place one foot close to the hands and extend the other so that the toes are just touching the ground. Kick up with the back leg and join the legs together above the head. Stretch up away from the hands. Practise continually until the position can be held without any wobble.

Although this is the simplest way to attain a handstand position, it is also the most difficult to control. If the initial kick is only slightly too vigorous the dive will overbalance before the diver is really ready.

Two Footed Take-off

This is slightly more difficult, but gives a more controlled balance position.

Start as for the kick up method, but with both feet close to the hands. Push both feet off so that the body goes through the tuck position into the vertical.

In the early stages, support at the hips may be essential. As strength develops, the legs may be kept straight throughout. This is called an 'elephant lift'.

Once the armstand balance position can be achieved, then the movements can be tried from the bathside.

Armstand Dive

Attain an armstand balance position on the poolside. Bring the head into line so that the body overbalances and then push off strongly with the arms to bring the shoulders back into line with the feet. From the bathside, head first entries may be all that is possible, but from the firmboard the arms should be brought into line with the body.

Remember - it is essential to overbalance before pushing off and also to keep the arms straight throughout the movement.

101. The diver starts with the hands close to the end of the board with the shoulders directly over the hands.

102.

103.

104.

102. The diver kicks up to a vertical position. A straight firm back is essential.

103. The position is held for as long as possible.

104-105. The diver overbalances slightly and then pushes off for an armstand dive.

105.

Armstand Back Fall

From the armstand balance position, let the head come into line with the body, keep the arms extended and overbalance. As the hands leave the side, bring them smartly down by the sides for a feet first entry.

From the poolside, it will be necessary to arch the back to get in feet first, but from the board the back should be kept straight and firm. Also from the bathside, keep the arms above the head for entry.

Emphasis should be put on a firm extension through the arms and body throughout the movement.

Armstand Somersault

Most single somersaults enter the water feet first, but because this movement starts in an armstand balance position, then entry will be head first.

Start in the balance position, allow the body to overbalance until about 30 degrees from the vertical, push strongly from the hands and bring the body into a tuck position. Keep looking over the knees for the point of entry. When this has been seen, extend the legs and stretch for entry.

This dive can also be performed using an open or closed pike position. It is executed in the same way except the legs remain straight throughout.

Remember, the tighter the body pikes the faster it will rotate.

106. From the balanced position

107. the diver tucks the head in, allows the feet to overbalance . . .

108. . . . and then pushes off hard from the board and then pikes ready for a head first entry.

OTHER DIVES

All the dives which can be performed from the springboard can also be performed from the highboard. Remember, the take-off must be adapted to get maximum height from the board and to get a safe distance from it.

5 LAND CONDITIONING

Many divers and coaches hold the belief that the only way to train to be a diver is by actually diving. As with any physical activity, the body must first be prepared so that it can meet the demands placed on it by that particular activity. This preparation is best done away from the pool in either a gymnasium, hall or outside on the grass. Land conditioning for divers is essential.

Even before a diving session, the body should be thoroughly warmed up. On a warm day the body may feel warm, but this is not sufficient. It must be put through a series of exercises which are designed to increase the flow of blood to the muscles, thereby reducing the risk of strains and pulls. Diving requires total concentration and this warming up session allows the diver to focus his attention on the work to be attempted. It is essential that both mind and body are prepared for the activity.

A perfect dive requires good posture, grace, strength, suppleness and co-ordination. Land conditioning programmes must be designed to work on each of these areas in turn. A diver will never be able to achieve perfection if any of these areas are lacking.

Correct posture is necessary for both the stance and the board prior to take-off and perhaps more importantly for the entry into the water. Many young divers, particularly girls, stand with very hollow backs. This must be discouraged and divers must learn to hold the body in a straight line. This correct posture is not only gained by tightening and relaxing muscles. The pelvis is the key to good posture. The bottom of the pelvis must be tipped under to bring the body truly into line. Muscles can then be tightened to hold this posture. This straight body position is particularly important for entries. Hollow back entries are weak and can lead to spinal injuries.

Suppleness is required if the diver is going to achieve good positions

109. Good posture with the pelvis tilted under and the stomach firm. Essential for the diver.

110. Ankle and foot extension is essential. Start with the hands close to the knees. Press the hips up high, ensuring that the toes remain curled under.

111. As skill develops, keep the hands and feet closer together.

112. Ankle turning also helps with flexibility.

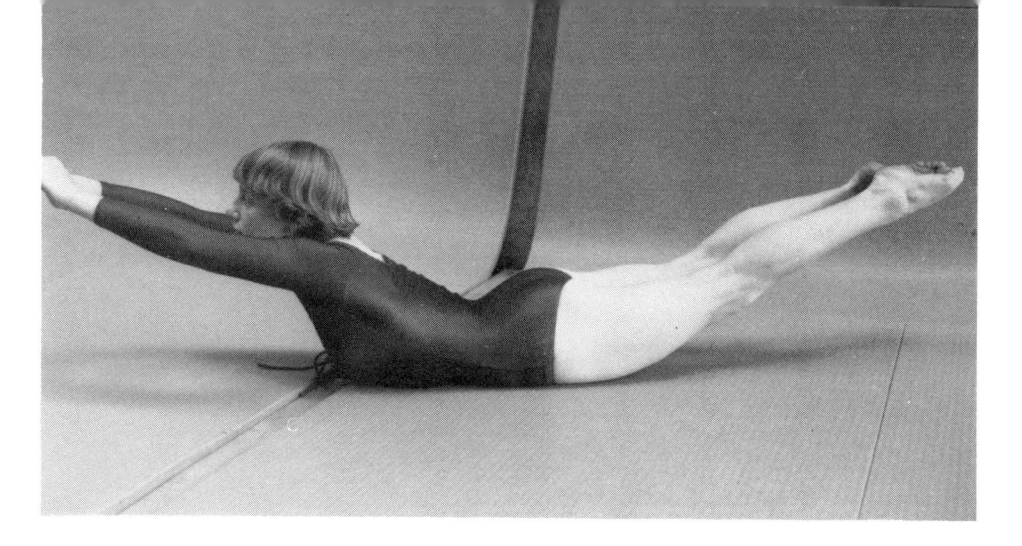

113. Back strength is essential for entries. Hold the position for a few seconds and then relax slowly.

during the flight through the air. Suppleness is achieved by putting the limbs through a greater range of movement than is usually achieved.

Strength is necessary particularly in the legs, arms, stomach and back. A diver does not require strength that builds enormous muscle bulk. He or she requires strength to lift the body at take-off and to control the body in flight. Expensive or specialist weight training equipment is not necessary to improve strength. Use of own body weight or the weight of a partner is usually all that is required. Partner work is fun and particularly useful for the young diver. Light weight work can also be beneficial, but this should only be undertaken with the guidance of an expert. Indiscriminate use of weights can do more harm than good.

Stamina training must also be included if the diver is to able to dive consistently through a complete session. Fatigue leads to deterioration of performance and a diver must be generally fit so that he can dive as well at the end of a training session as at the beginning. Improvement of stamina is best achieved through circuit training where the diver performs a series of exercises either for a set period of time or for a set number of repetitions. As stamina improves, either the time limit or the number of repetitions can be increased.

The diver must also pay attention to diet, general health and appearance.

A good diver must not only feel good, but it is essential that he looks good. A sun tan helps.

In this chapter it is not possible to show all the exercises which can be performed. Choose exercises which suit the individual diver. Ensure that all areas of the body are worked. Start at the head and work downwards.

Remember, always warm up before undertaking strenuous exercise.

114.

114 - 115. Mobility in the hips is essential for the pike position. Lift the rib cage high before folding over into the pike position. Flat feet help to stretch the backs of the legs.

115.

116 - 117. More exercises for hip mobility. Many divers are unable to achieve very close pike positions as they are stiff in this area of the body.

116.

117.

118. The handstand. The partner supports to allow the diver to feel the extended position. The body must be directly in line over the hands.

119. 'V' sits help the pike position. The partner helps by pressing against the legs and back. Ensure the back is kept straight and the knees locked.

120.

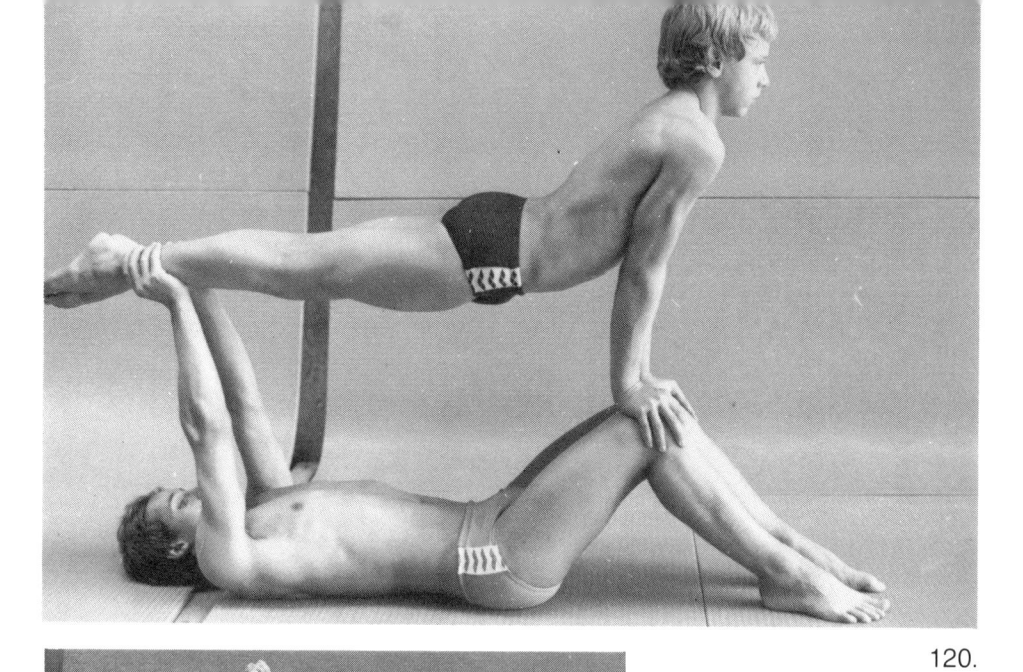

120 - 121. Partner activities make land conditioning fun. Ensure that partners are approximately the same weight.

121.

APPENDIX I

DEGREE OF DIFFICULTY

The degree of difficulty or tariff value is a number given to each dive which increases as the difficulty of the dive increases. They are used in the computation of a final score. The judges give their awards without taking into account the difficulty of the dive. The highest and the lowest scores are then cancelled and the remaining marks added together and then multiplied by the degree of difficulty to give the final score.

Examples of the degrees of difficulty are as follows:
A forward dive with tuck from the one metre board = 1.2
A forward dive straight from the one metre board = 1.4
The diver must therefore decide whether it is safer to execute the dive in the tuck position or risk the higher tariff (or more difficult) dive and hope that the marks will be almost the same.

The diver should always work towards the more difficult dive as eventually these should give the highest scores.

What the Judges are looking for

In any subjective sport it is sometimes difficult to see how a judge reached his award. Judges are given guidelines as to what to look for and a scale of marks which should be used. In the end, however, it is the judge's own opinion. Good judging only comes with experience. The judge is looking to see that all the basic requirements of the dive have been met. The rules state that the following points should be considered.

The run
The take-off
The technique and grace of the dive
   during the passage through the air

The entry into the water.

It is the grace during the flight which makes the dive aesthetically pleasing and is the difference between an average and a good diver.

The judge starts to mark from the starting position and the method of approach to this position should not be taken into consideration. It is advisable, however, to assume the position as smartly as possible as this creates the first impression and this is always important. The judge continues to observe until the whole body is completely below the surface of the water.

Judges mark in points on a scale from 0-10.

Completely failed	0 points
Unsatisfactory	½-2 points
Deficient	2½-4½ points
Satisfactory	5-6 points
Good	6½-8 points
Very good	8½-10 points

Ultimately it is the judge's own decision as to the correct category for a particular dive.

Penalties

There are certain penalties which are imposed by the referee when the diver makes certain mistakes.

If the diver performs a completely different dive, then a fail dive is declared. If it is performed in the wrong position then the highest award that can be given is two.

When a diver makes less than four contacts with the board, two points are deducted from each of the judge's awards.

In the execution of an armstand dive, if the diver fails to show a steady balance, then the judges deduct between one and three points. If he completely loses his balance and has to make a second attempt, then again two points are deducted from each of the judge's awards.

These are only a few of the penalties which may be deducted. A full list of the rules which govern diving competitions are to be found in the booklet, *The Organisation of a Diving Competition*, available from the ASA. This booklet also includes the degrees of difficulty for all the dives.

APPENDIX 2

DIVING AWARDS

Success in diving can be measured by the new dives that are mastered or the marks gained in competition. There are also diving awards which can be taken to measure achievement. The main aims of these proficiency awards are to give encouragement and to raise the standard of diving throughout the country. These awards start with the Star Awards which include both jumps and dives and progress to bronze, silver and gold standards. Silver and gold awards are available for both springboard and highboard.

The Star Awards

These dives must be performed from the bathside into water that is deeper than the height of the candidate with the arms extended above the head.

The examiners are looking for a good stance, some height in take-off, a recognisable position during flight and a neat entry. They are not looking for perfection, but a neat, recognisable dive.

Grade 1
1. A plain header
2. A forward dive, piked or with tuck
3. A back jump.

Grade 2
These dives must be performed from either a 1.30 metre firmboard or a one metre springboard into water that is at least 2.70 metres deep.
1. A plain header
2. A forward dive, piked or with tuck
3. An inward dive, piked or with tuck
4. A back dive, piked, with tuck or straight.

These awards can be examined by any holder of a diploma in physical education, an ASA Teacher's Certificate or Diving Teacher's Certificate, a County Diving Official or anyone who is approved by the ASA Diving Committee.

Details of the more advanced awards are available from the ASA, the address of which is given in Chapter 1.